j818.602 Rosenberg, Pam.
ROS
   Dinosaur jokes.

$22.79

DATE			

LAUGHING MATTERS

DINOSAUR JOKES

Compiled by Pam Rosenberg   Illustrated by Patrick Girouard

The Child's World®

Special thanks to Katie Cottrell for her assistance in compiling source materials.

Published in the United States of America by The Child's World®
P.O. Box 326, Chanhassen, MN 55317-0326
800-599-READ
www.childsworld.com

Acknowledgments
    The Child's World®: Mary Berendes, Publishing Director

    Editorial Directions, Inc.: E. Russell Primm, Editorial Director and
    Line Editor; Katie Marsico, Assistant Editor; Matthew Messbarger,
    Editorial Assistant; Susan Hindman and Susan Ashley, Proofreaders

    The Design Lab: Kathleen Petelinsek, Designer and Page Production

Registration

Library of Congress Cataloging-in-Publication Data
Rosenberg, Pam.
  Dinosaur jokes / compiled by Pam Rosenberg ; illustrated by Patrick
Girouard.
      p. cm. — (Laughing matters)
   Summary: Simple jokes and riddles about dinosaurs.
    ISBN 1-59296-073-1 (alk. paper)
   1. Dinosaurs—Juvenile humor. 2. Wit and humor, Juvenile. 3. Riddles,
Juvenile. [1. Dinosaurs—Humor. 2. Jokes. 3. Riddles.] I. Girouard, Patrick,
ill. II. Title. III. Series.
PN6231.D65 R63 2004
818'.602—dc22   2003018084

WHAT?

What's a dinosaur's curse?
A tyrannosaurus hex.

What's yellow on the outside and green on the inside?
A tyrannosaurus rex in a taxi.

What game does a tyrannosaurus rex like to play with humans?
Squash.

What does a tyrannosaurus rex eat?
Anything it wants.

What's the best way to talk to a tyrannosaurus rex?
Long distance.

What did the tyrannosaurus rex do after he drank all the water in Toronto?
He started to drink Canada Dry.

3

What age followed the Mesozoic Age?
The Clean-up-ozoic Age.

What did the dinosaur call her shirt-making business?
Try Sarah's Tops.

What was the fastest dinosaur?
The pronto-saurus.

What's as big as a dinosaur but weighs nothing?
A dinosaur's shadow.

What followed the dinosaur?
Its tail.

What did the cat say to the dinosaur?
Meow.

What should you do to a blue dinosaur?
Cheer it up.

What should you do if a dinosaur is sleeping in your bed? Sleep somewhere else.

What does a triceratops sit on? Its tricera-bottom.

5

What happened when the dinosaur walked through a corn field?
He made creamed corn.

What has a spiked tail, plates on its back, and sixteen wheels?
A stegosaurus on roller skates.

What goes "ha ha ha ha ha ha plop"?
A brontosaurus laughing its head off.

What's better than a talking dinosaur?
A spelling bee.

What dinosaur loves pancakes?
A tri-syrup-tops.

What was the fossil hunter doing during her final week at school?
Boning up for her final exams.

What did dinosaurs have that no other animal had?
Baby dinosaurs.

What do dinosaurs use for
the floors of their homes?
  Rep-tiles.

What's huge and bumps into
the sides of mountains?
  A brachiosaur playing
  Blind Man's Bluff.

What should you do if you see a
tyrannosaurus rex?
  Hope that it doesn't see you.

What should you do if a dinosaur sneezes?
  Get out of the way.

What dinosaur would you find in a rodeo?
  A bronco-saurus.

What makes more noise than a dinosaur?
  Two dinosaurs.

What kind of tool does a prehistoric reptile use?
  A dino-saw.

WHAT DO YOU CALL?

What do you call a dinosaur that left its armor out in the rain?
A stegosau-rust.

What do you call a leaky dinosaur?
A bronto-porous.

What do you call a plated dinosaur when it is asleep?
Stego-snorus.

What do you call a person brave enough to stick his right hand into the mouth of a diplodocus?
Lefty.

9

What do you call a tyrannosaurus rex when it wears a cowboy hat and boots?
    Tyrannosaurus tex.

What do you call an allosaurus that isn't feeling well?
    An illosaurus.

What do you call a dinosaur that's as tall as a house, with long, sharp teeth, and 12 claws on each foot?
    Sir.

What do you call a fossil that doesn't want to work?
    Lazy bones.

What do you call a dinosaur that crosses the road, rolls in dirt, and crosses the road again?
    A dirty double crosser.

What do you call a dinosaur with no eyes?
    Anything you want, he can't see you.

What do you call a dinosaur playing hide-and-seek?
    Doyouthinkhesaurus.

WHAT DO YOU GET?

What do you get when you cross a stegosaurus with a cow?
Milk that's too scary to drink!

What do you get when two dinosaurs get into a car accident?
Tyrannosaurus wrecks.

What do you get when you cross a dinosaur with fireworks?
Dino-mite.

What do you get if you cross a Triceratops with a kangaroo?
Tricera-hops.

What would you get if a herd of dinosaurs ran over Batman and Robin?
Flatman and Ribbon.

What do you get when you cross a dinosaur with a parrot?

I don't know but when it asks for a cracker you'd better give it one!

What do you get if you cross a mouse with a triceratops?

Huge holes in the baseboards.

What do you get if you cross a dinosaur with a mole?

A very big hole in your garden.

What do you get when you cross a dinosaur with a skunk?

A big stinker!

What do you get if you cross a pig with a dinosaur?

Jurassic pork.

What do you get if a dinosaur walks through a strawberry patch?

Strawberry jam.

HOW?

How did iguanadons catch flies?
With their baseball mitts.

How do you get milk and eggs from a dinosaur?
Steal its shopping cart.

How do you know if there's a dinosaur under your bed?
You need a ladder to climb in.

How do you know if a dinosaur is under your bed?
You bump your nose on the ceiling.

How do you stop a charging dinosaur?
Take away its credit cards.

How do you ask a dinosaur to lunch?
Tea, Rex?

How can you tell if there is a dinosaur in your refrigerator?
The door won't close.

How do you get down from a dinosaur?
    You don't. You get down from a goose.

How many dinosaurs can fit in an empty box?
    One. After that, the box isn't empty anymore.

How fast should you run when a dinosaur is chasing you?
    One step faster than the dinosaur.

How do dinosaurs pay their bills?
    With tyrannosaurus checks.

How did the dinosaur feel after she ate a pillow?
    Down in the mouth.

How do you make a dinosaur float?
    Put a scoop of ice cream in a glass of root beer and add one dinosaur!

DID YOU HEAR?

Did you hear about the tyrannosaurus rex who entertained a lot?
He always had friends for lunch.

WHERE?

Where did the velociraptor buy things?
At the dino-store.

Where do dinosaurs get their mail?
At the dead-letter office.

KNOCK-KNOCK:

Knock knock.
Who's there?
Ron.
Ron who?
Ron a little faster, I see a dinosaur over there!

Knock knock.
Who's there?
Dinosaur.
Dinosaur who?
Dinosaur that you didn't invite her to the party.

Knock knock.
Who's there?
Dozen.
Dozen who?
Dozen anyone around here know how to spell pterodactyl?

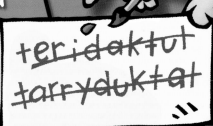

teridaktul
tarryduktal

17

WHY?

Why did the dinosaur cross the road?
So she could eat the chickens on the other side.

Why did the dinosaur get in the bed?
Because he was tired.

Why did the dinosaur cross the road?
Because it was the chicken's day off.

Why do dinosaurs paint their toenails red?
So they can hide in a strawberry patch.

Why did the dinosaur cross the road?
Because the chicken hadn't evolved yet.

Why did the stegosaurus go to night school?
He wanted to be able to read in the dark.

Why do dinosaurs eat raw meat?
Because they don't know how to cook.

18

Why did the stegosaurus run around and around his bed?
  He was trying to catch up on his sleep.

Why don't the dinosaurs let the stegosaurus play baseball with them?
  He's always spiking the other players.

Why did the dinosaur put on a bandage?
  She had a dino-sore.

Why did the apatosaurus devour the factory?
  Because she was a plant eater.

Why are there old dinosaur bones in the museum?
  Because they can't afford new ones.

Why didn't the tyrannosaurus rex skeleton attack the museum visitors?
  Because he had no guts.

Why was the dinosaur afraid of the ocean?
  Because there was something fishy about it.

WHEN?

When can three dinosaurs get under an umbrella and not get wet?
When it isn't raining.

WHO?

Who was the first dog dinosaur?
Terrier-dactyl.

WHICH?

Who makes the best prehistoric reptile clothes?
A dino-sewer.

Which dinosaur has three horns and three wheels?
Tricycle-tops.

Which kind of dinosaur can jump higher than a house?
Any kind—a house can't jump!

MISCELLANEOUS:

Billy Brontosaurus: I think we just stepped in quicksand.
Betty Brontosaurus: I'm getting that sinking feeling too!

Customer: Why is there a tyrannosaurus rex in my soup?
Waiter: The chef ran out of flies.

Customer: Waiter!
Waiter: Yes?
Customer: What's this brontosaurus doing in my soup?
Waiter: Looks like the backstroke.

Customer: What's the hardest part about making dinosaur soup?
Chef: Stirring it!

Jake: I lost my pet dinosaur.
Sarah: Why don't you put an ad in the newspaper?
Jake: What good would that do? He can't read!

22

Teacher: Name ten dinosaurs in ten seconds.
Student: OK, eight iguanadons and two stegosaurus.

Mom: Why are you crying?
Daniel: Because I wanted to get a dinosaur for my baby brother.
Mom: That's no reason to cry.
Daniel: Yes it is. No one would trade me!

Katie: I can lift a dinosaur with one hand.
Carl: I don't believe you.
Katie: Get me a dinosaur with one hand and I'll prove it!

Emily: Is it true that a dinosaur won't attack if you're holding a tree branch?
Paul: That depends on how fast you carry it!

23

About Patrick Girouard:

Patrick Girouard has been illustrating books for almost 15 years but still looks remarkably lifelike. He loves reading, movies, coffee, robots, a beautiful red-haired lady named Rita, and especially his sons, Marc and Max. Here's an interesting fact: A dog named Sam lives under his drawing board. You can visit him (Patrick, not Sam) at www.pgirouard.com.

About Pam Rosenberg:

Pam Rosenberg is a former junior high school teacher and corporate trainer. She currently works as an author, editor, and the mother of Sarah and Jake. She took on this project as a service to all her fellow parents of young children. At least now their kids will have lots of jokes to choose from when looking for the one they will tell their parents over and over and over again!